Enid and the Church Fire

By Cynthia G. Williams

Illustrated by Betty Harper

Published in 1999
by Broadman & Holman Publishers, Nashville, Tennessee

Printed in the United States of America
All rights reserved
ISBN 0-8054-1885-7
Art direction and design by Jennifer Davidson

Scripture quotations are from the *King James Version*.

Library of Congress Cataloging-in-Publication Data

Williams, Cynthia G., 1958-
    Enid and the church fire / Cynthia G. Williams ; illustrated by
      Betty Harper.
        p.   cm. -- (Our neighborhood)
    ISBN 0-8054-1885-7
    [1. Fires Ficton.   2. Christian life Fiction.   3. Afro-Americans
        Fiction.]   I. Harper, Betty, ill.   II. Title.   III. Series:
Williams, Cynthia G., 1958-   Our neighborhood.
PZ7.W6559235En   1999
[Fic] --dc21
                                 99-29301
                                   CIP

1 2 3 4 5 03 02 01 00 99

BROADMAN
&HOLMAN
PUBLISHERS

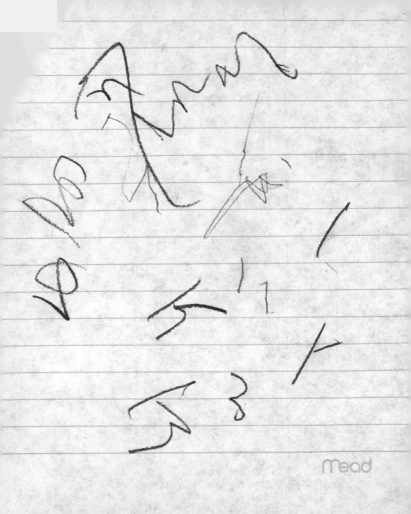

She's been there for me through breakdowns, breakthroughs, breakups. . .
and even an occasional break-a-leg as my former news producer.
But mostly she's been there from the beginning when "Enid" was just
a blank space I stared at on my computer screen.
I dedicate book two to my friend Jill who put the word "end" in friend,
because she says that's how long she'll be there for me.

Cynthia G. Williams

*Train up a child in the way he should go: and when he is old,
he will not depart from it.*
(Proverbs 22: 6, KJV)

It was nighttime, but the raging fire lit up Enid's neighborhood.

"Call the station for another truck!" the fire captain shouted. "This is going to be a tough one to put out."

Enid stood behind the yellow caution tape with Grandma and her friends. They watched in disbelief as the church Grandma had attended for years went up in flames. The steeple was the only part of the church not yet destroyed by the smoke and flames that poured out of every window.

"Get that crowd back!" shouted the fire captain, holding a radio in one hand and a bullhorn in the other.

"It's Captain Mel," Enid said to her friends.

"It sure is," Ron acknowledged. "He was just at school last week talking about fire safety."

Ment got up on his tiptoes and waved, but Captain Mel was busy with his crew fighting the flames from the burning church.

A loud crash startled the kids. They watched as the steeple gave way to the roaring flames.

"Lord have mercy! How could this have happened?" Grandma was crying.

Enid reached out to hold her hand. "It'll be okay, Grandma."

"I know, child. A church is just a building, but oh, the sweet memories I have from all those years. I just can't watch anymore, Enid honey. Let's go home."

J ust as Enid and Grandma started to walk away, someone called out, "Hey, wait a second."

It was Captain Mel. He had made his way underneath the yellow tape to tell Enid hello. "How are you holding up?"

"Okay, I guess, Captain Mel, but Grandma's not doing so well."

"Do you have any idea how the fire started?" Grandma asked.

"Not yet, ma'am, but we're searching for clues."

"Did somebody set it on purpose?" Enid asked.

"We don't know right now whether someone set it on purpose or whether it was accidental."

"You're needed over here, Captain!" The urgent request broke into their conversation.

"I've got to go now. The fire fighters need me," he said.

As Captain Mel left to go, Enid took one last look at the burning church. It was only yesterday when it stood strong and tall, and Enid and her friends were happily playing in Sunday school.

I need more glue!" Enid looked up from her project only long enough to make a request. She always liked Sunday school, even better than normal school. There was no math at Sunday school, and she enjoyed hearing the Bible stories every week.

"Mrs. Wilson, why did Joseph's brothers treat him so mean?" Enid asked.

Today's story had been about Joseph and his coat of many colors.

Enid and her classmates were busy cutting multi-colored ribbons to wear in next Sunday's play about Joseph.

Mrs. Wilson answered, "It's because they were jealous of him."

"Did they know he'd be governor one day?" Enid was cutting more pieces of ribbon to paste onto the cardboard cutout.

"No, they didn't, Enid."

"But when he became governor, he forgave them for being mean to him," stated Enid.

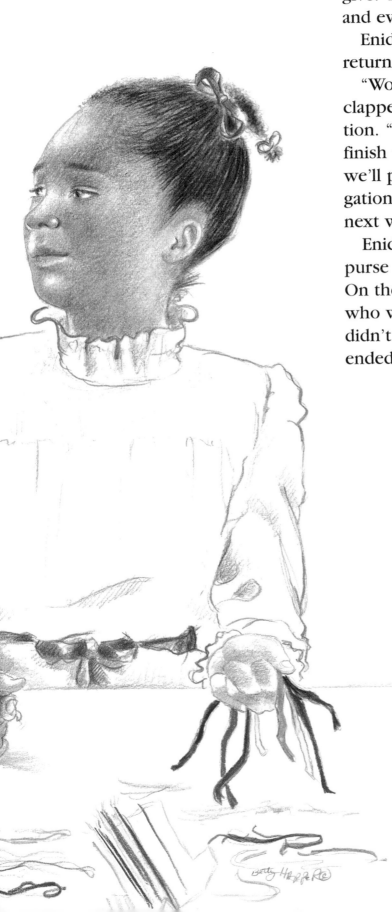

Forgiveness is important, Enid. The Bible says we need to be forgiven and learn to forgive. That applies to kids, parents, teachers, and everyone else," Mrs. Wilson smiled.

Enid was pleased with this explanation and returned to work on her ribbons.

"Workshop time is over!" Mrs. Wilson clapped her hands to bring the class to attention. "Be sure to take your ribbons home and finish them there if you need to. Remember, we'll perform our play for the entire congregation immediately following Sunday school next week."

Enid cleaned up her ribbons, gathered her purse and book bag, and headed for the door. On the way home she saw her friend Vi, who was playing a game of hopscotch. Enid didn't mind that Vi's church service always ended before hers.

Hey, Enid, want to play?"

"Can't right now. I've got to go home, change clothes, and eat dinner. But maybe later."

"Okay, I'll walk with you," said Vi.

Enid handed Vi her book bag while she reached into her tiny purse for the brightly colored ribbon.

"Oh, no!"

"Oh no, what?" asked Vi.

"I must have left it back in the Sunday school room," Enid sighed.

"Left what?"

"We've got to run back, Vi. I'll tell you on the way," Enid said.

The two took off running as fast as they could to Enid's church.

The church parking lot was empty, but sitting near the curb Enid saw a familiar truck. Then she spotted Mr. Moore, the maintenance man. Enid and Vi ran to catch him before he got in his truck.

"Mr. Moore!" Enid called, struggling to catch her breath. "I left my Joseph's ribbon in my room, and I need to take it home to finish for next Sunday's play. I've just got to get it. I know where it is and..."

"Now hold on there, Enid," said Mr. Moore. He could see how much the ribbon meant to her. "Don't worry about a thing. I've got the key. We'll go in and get your ribbon."

"Thank you, Mr. Moore!" Enid said.

The threesome then walked up to the church entrance and Mr. Moore unlocked the door. "Now don't y'all stay long. I'll be waiting here for you."

"We won't," Enid called as she and Vi ran through the church sanctuary and out a side door that led to the Sunday school rooms.

Look Vi, here it is!"

"Here what is?" asked Vi.

"It's my ribbon for next Sunday's play about Joseph. Isn't it pretty?"

"Sure, it's real nice. Now, let's go before we get in trouble."

As the two headed for the door, Enid stopped.

"Now what?" Vi asked.

"Don't you smell that?"

"Smell what?"

"It smells like... I don't know. It just smells funny," Enid said.

"This church is old, girl. No telling what you smell. Let's go before Mr. Moore comes looking for us."

The day after the fire, the yellow caution tape was the only thing left standing. The church had burned completely to the ground. Fire fighters poked around in the ashes, and a reporter was sitting on a nearby curb writing something. Enid and her friends approached him.

Enid wondered if the reporter could tell them how the fire started. He looked up when she and her friends walked over to where he was sitting.

"How are you kids doing?" he asked. "Was this your church?"

"It was my church," Enid answered. "Any idea how it started?"

"No, not yet. It's still under investigation. The FBI has been asked to help because of all the church burnings that have happened recently."

"You mean somebody probably did this on purpose?" Enid asked.

"I'm not saying that, but it's a theory," the reporter replied.

"What's a theory?" asked Vi.

"Well, it's what you think might have happened, but it hasn't been proven yet. I'd like to talk to you kids some more, but I'm doing another story about this fire and I've got a deadline."

A few minutes later the four friends were at Mr. Jemison's store. Chester and some of the other men, who always hung around the store, were outside talking about the fire.

"I hope they throw the person who started that fire in jail!" Chester said angrily. He and the other men seemed mad about the church burning.

"Yeah, times are really gettin' bad when the church ain't even a safe place to be anymore," one man said.

"But they don't know how the fire started, do they?" Enid's question made the men stop talking and look at her.

"Well, they don't know what started it yet, but it doesn't look good," another of the men answered.

Chester got up from the step and moved closer to Enid and her friends.

"Y'all are too young to understand how some people can just be bad," he said. "Take it from old Chester, people do mean things, even to churches."

"Well, even if that's true, shouldn't we forgive them?" Enid asked.

"Forgive them?" Chester made a face. "We should think about puttin' them in jail."

All the men agreed.

"Maybe so, but people forgive mean things too," Enid said.

With that the four friends walked inside Mr. Jemison's store to buy ice cream treats.

That night at home, Enid watched the news with her mother and grandmother. The reporter she had talked to was doing a story about the fire.

"Right now, the fire is under investigation," he said. "Officials aren't commenting on the cause of the blaze. They did say something doesn't smell right about the fire that completely destroyed a historic neighborhood church."

Enid jumped up. "A smell, that's it!" she exclaimed.

"What's it?" Grandma asked.

"Well, me and Vi went back to the church Sunday after I'd left my ribbon in Sunday school. When we were coming out of the church, we smelled something."

"I should call the fire captain in the morning and let him know you smelled something," Enid's grandmother said.

The next Sunday, Enid and her class performed their play in the parking lot of the burned-down church. They had a larger audience than they had expected. The fire brought out the television cameras and city officials from all over.

"Wow, look at all these people," one of her classmates whispered to Enid.

"That's okay, don't be nervous. Just do it like we practiced."

Enid adjusted her badge of brightly colored ribbons. All the kids in her class wore a badge shaped like Joseph's coat of many colors. Hidden behind the badge was a secret message the kids had chosen. In the final scene of the play, the children turned over their badges and everyone proudly displayed this message: Forgive, Forget, Move Forward.

After the play, Captain Mel pulled Enid and her friends to the side.

"I wanted you to be the first to hear the news," he said.

"About the fire?" they asked excitedly.

"Yes," said the captain. "We're pretty sure the fire was electrical. That means it started as the result of faulty or old wiring in the church."

"Nobody set it on purpose?" Enid asked.

"We don't think so, Enid. And your telling us about that odd smell helped us complete our investigation."

"Wow, Enid girl, you're a detective!" Vi said.

Enid and her friends laughed.

"That's good news," Enid said. "Grandma said it's easier for people to build a new church building than for them to build trust and learn forgiveness."

"Your grandma's one smart lady," said Captain Mel.

"I guess it runs in the family," Enid said with a smile.

Reflections for Adults

Adults can learn many things from children, as we see in this story of Enid. Children are very perceptive, not only to real-life dangers, like the smoke from a fire, but also to the nature of people that keeps us from forgiving one another.

As a parent, grandparent, teacher, guardian, or friend, you can never talk to children enough.

Encourage the children in your life to talk with you about their questions and concerns.

Take the time to listen. You might learn something. You might even save a life.

Added to this important lesson is one we learn from the Bible. It is simple, but timeless.

And whoso shall receive one such little child in my name receiveth me.
(Matthew 18:5, KJV)